"Sometimes we've been to four different countries in four days. It sounds glamorous when you read about it, but it's actually very hard work. When we went over to Germany for three days recently we started work at nine in the morning and didn't stop 'til midnight. But it's something we know we have to do. We're thankful that people like us so much."

"All I want is for the band to be as good on stage as we are in the studio. At the end of the day, touring's what it's all about. We're constantly growing and doing new things, but most importantly I think the five of us are now better friends than we ever were."

"One of my ambitions was always to perform in front of royalty, so when we performed in front of Princess Margaret at the Royal Variety Performance that was pretty lucky. She was great, she said to us 'Well done, I heard lots of screams from the young girls'."

"People tend to spill their problems on me. I know I don't have all the answers but I'm a good agony aunt."

"Madonna's too masculine for me. It might sound a bit sexist, but I like women with nice curves and long hair – Kylie Minogue types."

"We know that it's important for us to be successful in other countries, but we will certainly never desert Britain and our wonderful fans here. We have worked so hard to get them and they are so loyal that we don't want to do anything to disappoint them. We think about them all the time."

"I'm convinced the world could blow up any day. I think everything is going sadly wrong with the world. Everyone knows about the ozone layer, but there's so many other things going on. We've abused the world so much."

"We have relationships while we're away. You know, we're young lads…"

"I remember when I used to have to be somewhere in the morning by 8.30. I would never wake up until 8.30. I can't help it – I love my bed!"

"I get quite emotional at the beginning of a tour, especially on the first night. When I'm back stage waiting to go on and I can hear the fans already going wild, it actually brings tears to my eyes."

"We're good-looking lads and we frolic on stage, but we've still got our own personalities."

"I never knew I would be doing something like this, but I should have been prepared for it because both my parents are very musical. I guess I must have got my dancing ability from my father, who earned a lot of medals for his dancing."

"Once I fall in love, I fall in love very deeply and I think that to be in a relationship like that and to spend so much time away from a girl would be unbearable and unfair for both of us. But the way things are right now, if I was to meet the right girl I would never find out if she was the right one because I wouldn't be able to spend enough time with her."

howard donald

"I dream a lot. I find if I can't get to sleep for ages, when I do drop off I'll have a dream. The worst dream was when I woke up and I thought me hands were growing. Another terrible one was, I shut my eyes and there were all these bad colours in my mind – making noises and flashing. You know what it could be, I don't remember much about me mum and dad's divorce. I think I was about eight when they divorced but I think something happened that I can't remember. And it comes out in me dreams."

"Groups think drugs might help them cope. But it's a false belief. In the end they wreck your life. We have never taken them and we never would."

"I put myself down a lot because I don't think I'm good looking but I don't think I'm ugly either. On this, I think just the same as Mark, that the way you feel and project yourself as a performer matters just as much."

"If you think about what we were two years ago compared to now it's unbelievable. Suddenly we're stars... I think that's why we are so down to earth because it could end. I'll definitely make sure that I stay normal. I know there are definitely a few people in the band that could change and I know who they are but I'm not telling you. But we'll try to keep 'em normal."

"I believe in life after death but I don't think I've been reincarnated. I believe in Heaven but I don't believe in Hell. I can't imagine myself just dying and that's it. There has to be more. I wouldn't mind coming back as a pair of knickers – Cindy Crawford's knickers."

"People who say we're manufactured really don't know what we're about. We write most of our own material and we do all our own choreography. We're in control when it comes to our music and our look. We always want to keep our ideas and our music fresh – that's important for us if we want to keep moving ahead."

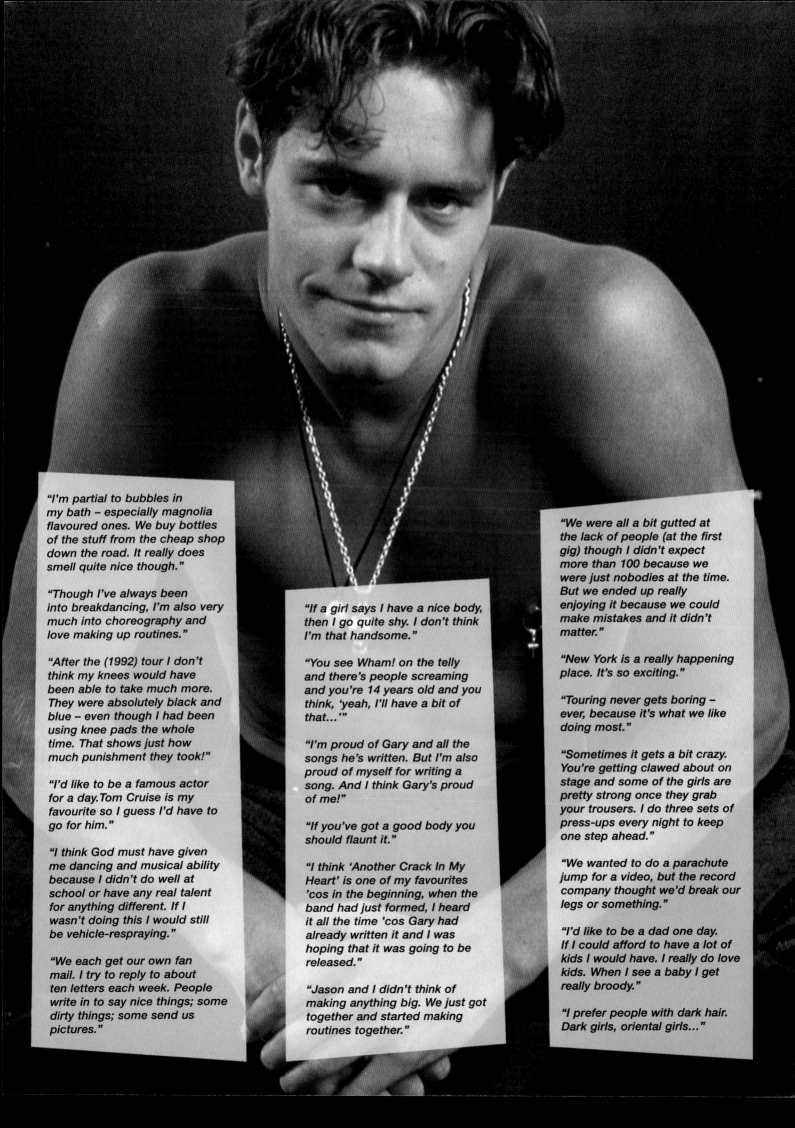

"I'm partial to bubbles in my bath – especially magnolia flavoured ones. We buy bottles of the stuff from the cheap shop down the road. It really does smell quite nice though."

"Though I've always been into breakdancing, I'm also very much into choreography and love making up routines."

"After the (1992) tour I don't think my knees would have been able to take much more. They were absolutely black and blue – even though I had been using knee pads the whole time. That shows just how much punishment they took!"

"I'd like to be a famous actor for a day. Tom Cruise is my favourite so I guess I'd have to go for him."

"I think God must have given me dancing and musical ability because I didn't do well at school or have any real talent for anything different. If I wasn't doing this I would still be vehicle-respraying."

"We each get our own fan mail. I try to reply to about ten letters each week. People write in to say nice things; some dirty things; some send us pictures."

"If a girl says I have a nice body, then I go quite shy. I don't think I'm that handsome."

"You see Wham! on the telly and there's people screaming and you're 14 years old and you think, 'yeah, I'll have a bit of that...'"

"I'm proud of Gary and all the songs he's written. But I'm also proud of myself for writing a song. And I think Gary's proud of me!"

"If you've got a good body you should flaunt it."

"I think 'Another Crack In My Heart' is one of my favourites 'cos in the beginning, when the band had just formed, I heard it all the time 'cos Gary had already written it and I was hoping that it was going to be released."

"Jason and I didn't think of making anything big. We just got together and started making routines together."

"We were all a bit gutted at the lack of people (at the first gig) though I didn't expect more than 100 because we were just nobodies at the time. But we ended up really enjoying it because we could make mistakes and it didn't matter."

"New York is a really happening place. It's so exciting."

"Touring never gets boring – ever, because it's what we like doing most."

"Sometimes it gets a bit crazy. You're getting clawed about on stage and some of the girls are pretty strong once they grab your trousers. I do three sets of press-ups every night to keep one step ahead."

"We wanted to do a parachute jump for a video, but the record company thought we'd break our legs or something."

"I'd like to be a dad one day. If I could afford to have a lot of kids I would have. I really do love kids. When I see a baby I get really broody."

"I prefer people with dark hair. Dark girls, oriental girls..."

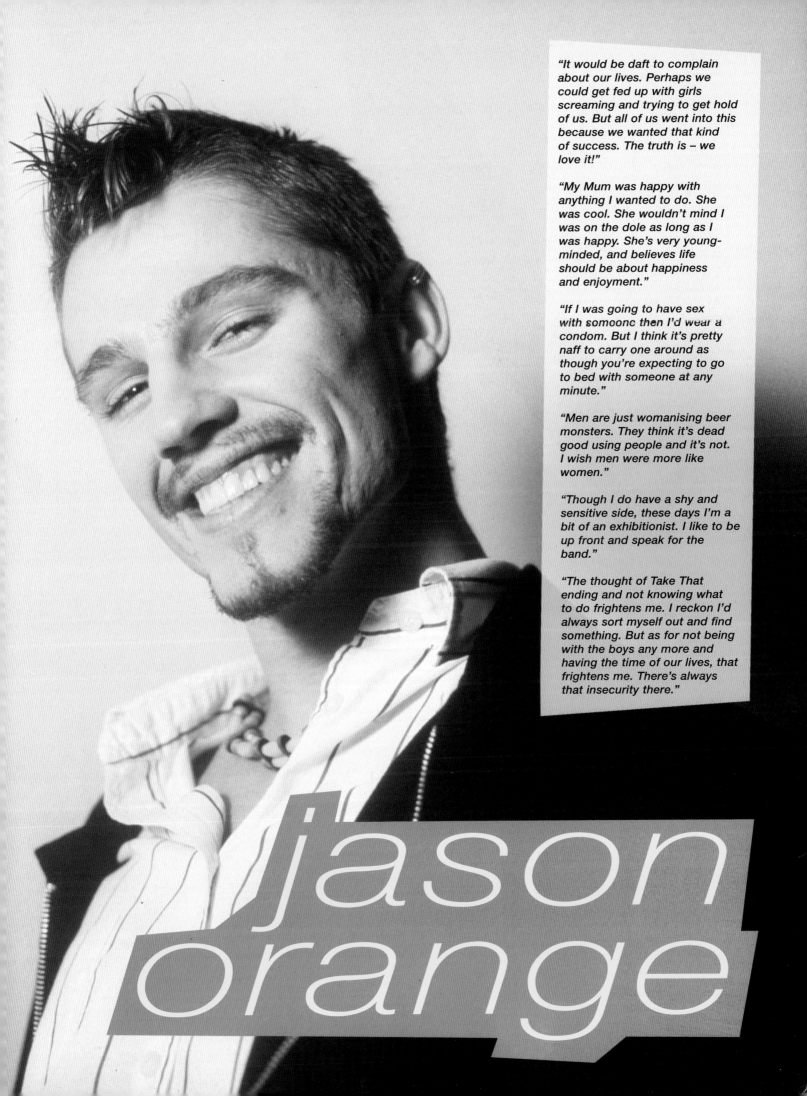

"It would be daft to complain about our lives. Perhaps we could get fed up with girls screaming and trying to get hold of us. But all of us went into this because we wanted that kind of success. The truth is – we love it!"

"My Mum was happy with anything I wanted to do. She was cool. She wouldn't mind I was on the dole as long as I was happy. She's very young-minded, and believes life should be about happiness and enjoyment."

"If I was going to have sex with someone then I'd wear a condom. But I think it's pretty naff to carry one around as though you're expecting to go to bed with someone at any minute."

"Men are just womanising beer monsters. They think it's dead good using people and it's not. I wish men were more like women."

"Though I do have a shy and sensitive side, these days I'm a bit of an exhibitionist. I like to be up front and speak for the band."

"The thought of Take That ending and not knowing what to do frightens me. I reckon I'd always sort myself out and find something. But as for not being with the boys any more and having the time of our lives, that frightens me. There's always that insecurity there."

jason orange

"I used to read everything but it's not a big deal any more. I just know that I won't have said a lot of what I'm quoted to have said."

"Del Boy and Rodney from Only Fools And Horses are really brilliant, dead funny. Because it's really about brotherhood, I think that is the thing that appeals to me. The brothers and the Grandad sitting in the corner talking about the war reminds me of our family when we were growing up."

"I was totally different a year ago to what I am now. And I know that in the next few years I am going to change more and more. Being in a band like this just can't help but change you. You meet so many people, see so many things – you can't help but learn and be influenced by everything around you."

"We look at what we do not so much as pervy, but as sexual."

"I got that jacket, then Howard bought this sequinned codpiece. We got so much stick for that look but it worked! We were just doing our thing!"

"I pray a lot... I pray for happiness, the underprivileged and the homeless."

"We're just out to shock. We'll do whatever it takes – we're here to have a good time."

"I don't particularly dislike any type of music but I do dislike too much of one type."

"I believe that you should look after your body, and because of that it's important what you put into it. I like to eat fresh food, food which is packed with vitamins."

"We have a crowd who follow us everywhere and it's nice to see familiar faces."

"I recently bought a big map of the world and put it on my bedroom wall. I've never been interested in the world before. There's a big world out there."

"We're all young and have good bodies which we're proud of. So why go on stage and cover them up? Let's get sexy!"

"I am one of those people who just likes to write their feelings about life down. I write down various things that I have been thinking about in the form of poetry. Maybe one day I'll have them published in a limited edition."

"Do what you want to do and not what everyone else wants you to do. So many people will try to influence you, but you'll only find happiness from within yourself."

"I've wasted a lot of time in my life. I'm only realising now what's going down."

"I think the touch of skin is just wonderful. Dancing can be just like sex, you enjoy your body and enjoy each other. I try to be sexually powerful when I'm dancing."

"I used to be a Mormon when I was about six or seven. All our family were, but they aren't any more. We still pray, though."

"I'm not afraid of losing my masculinity because I know it's there. I don't have to prove I'm a man."

"I don't like wearing anything in bed, not even pants. There are always ways of keeping warm. If it's really cold I'll just put another quilt on."

"We set ourselves a series of aims and made rules to get there. To be totally successful you have to be single-minded. Girlfriends didn't come into it."

"I'm gonna marry someone I'm attracted to because of what they are, not what they look like."

"It was cold in New York, really freezing. It was a good trip because we got to see some of the sights. We even went on a boat to see the Statue Of Liberty and she was lovely! I really liked it over there."

"I think I must have upset some of the older pupils at school because though I was younger than them I was always getting the big parts – the parts that the older guys thought they should get."

"I had my driving test on the day of a photo shoot for Smash Hits. I did the pictures first and then had my test. I wasn't really nervous because I knew that my driving was okay but I thought I'd fail on my Highway Code. Gaz was being really good, he was testing me on my code. After I passed I drove back to another photo session and I was late and everyone shouted at me."

"There's been lots of girls I've liked the look of, but when I've got to know them I went straight off them. Now I know it's personality. I like someone who can make me laugh. I don't mean tell jokes, but someone who can have a good time and mess about a bit. Someone who's game for a laugh."

mark owen

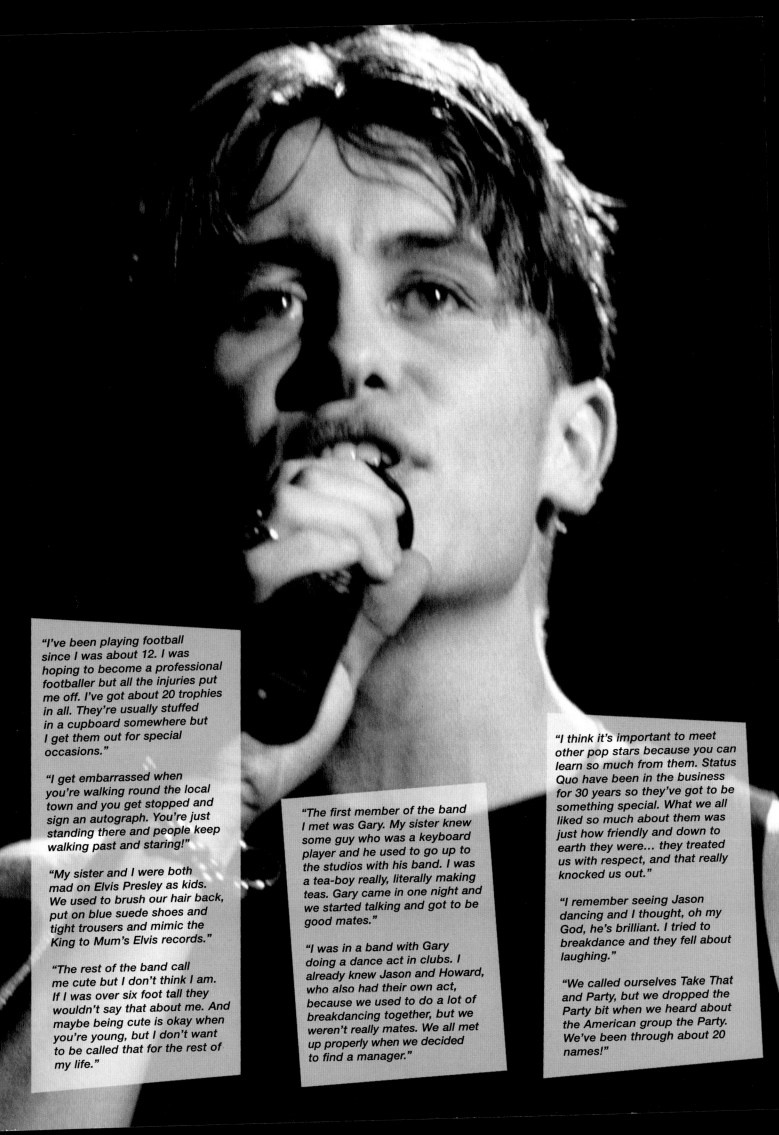

"I've been playing football since I was about 12. I was hoping to become a professional footballer but all the injuries put me off. I've got about 20 trophies in all. They're usually stuffed in a cupboard somewhere but I get them out for special occasions."

"I get embarrassed when you're walking round the local town and you get stopped and sign an autograph. You're just standing there and people keep walking past and staring!"

"My sister and I were both mad on Elvis Presley as kids. We used to brush our hair back, put on blue suede shoes and tight trousers and mimic the King to Mum's Elvis records."

"The rest of the band call me cute but I don't think I am. If I was over six foot tall they wouldn't say that about me. And maybe being cute is okay when you're young, but I don't want to be called that for the rest of my life."

"The first member of the band I met was Gary. My sister knew some guy who was a keyboard player and he used to go up to the studios with his band. I was a tea-boy really, literally making teas. Gary came in one night and we started talking and got to be good mates."

"I was in a band with Gary doing a dance act in clubs. I already knew Jason and Howard, who also had their own act, because we used to do a lot of breakdancing together, but we weren't really mates. We all met up properly when we decided to find a manager."

"I think it's important to meet other pop stars because you can learn so much from them. Status Quo have been in the business for 30 years so they've got to be something special. What we all liked so much about them was just how friendly and down to earth they were... they treated us with respect, and that really knocked us out."

"I remember seeing Jason dancing and I thought, oh my God, he's brilliant. I tried to breakdance and they fell about laughing."

"We called ourselves Take That and Party, but we dropped the Party bit when we heard about the American group the Party. We've been through about 20 names!"

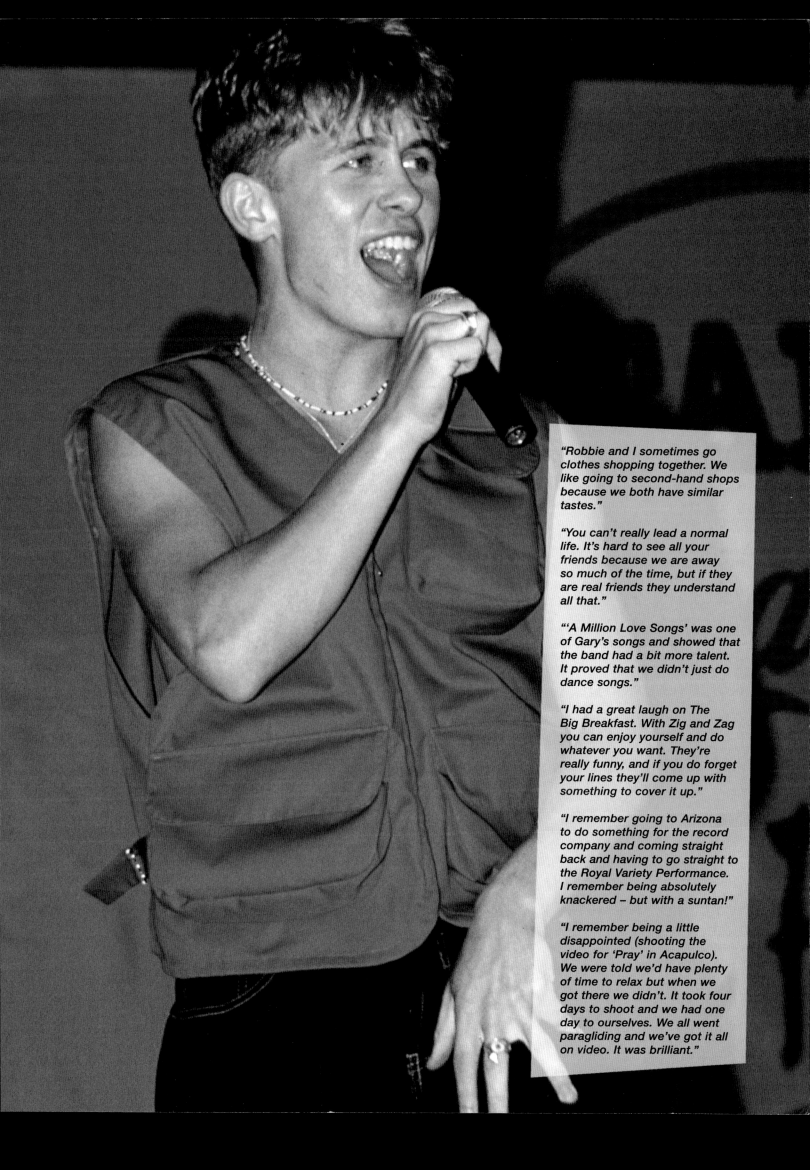

"Robbie and I sometimes go clothes shopping together. We like going to second-hand shops because we both have similar tastes."

"You can't really lead a normal life. It's hard to see all your friends because we are away so much of the time, but if they are real friends they understand all that."

"'A Million Love Songs' was one of Gary's songs and showed that the band had a bit more talent. It proved that we didn't just do dance songs."

"I had a great laugh on The Big Breakfast. With Zig and Zag you can enjoy yourself and do whatever you want. They're really funny, and if you do forget your lines they'll come up with something to cover it up."

"I remember going to Arizona to do something for the record company and coming straight back and having to go straight to the Royal Variety Performance. I remember being absolutely knackered – but with a suntan!"

"I remember being a little disappointed (shooting the video for 'Pray' in Acapulco). We were told we'd have plenty of time to relax but when we got there we didn't. It took four days to shoot and we had one day to ourselves. We all went paragliding and we've got it all on video. It was brilliant."

"The feeling of having a Number One with 'Pray' is just too difficult to describe. But we certainly did some partying to celebrate…"

"I was nervous about doing 'Babe' live for the first time because you never know how people will react. After a minute, I could see the girls in the front row crying. It was a very emotional sight. I had to bite my lip to keep control."

"I take multi-vitamin tablets every day. I find that ensures I get every supplement and vitamin I need. But I don't really like to preach about healthy eating… I think it's each to his own belief."

"When a girl walks past and you smell her scent, the aroma cloud that follows is the best smell in the world."

"My Mum was wary about me becoming part of a pop group at first... Now I think she gets more excited than most of our fans when she goes to shows! She loves the band and our music."

"I worry about the rest of the group. I'm always making sure everyone's got their bag and all their bits. I think it annoys the others."

"Our fans are amazing. They follow us everywhere – they turn up when you least expect it. They're very dedicated."

"I actually fall in love every day. I believe that eventually everyone meets the right person, but along the way you meet a lot of people who aren't right and that's when it hurts. Somewhere there's a girl for me."

"As long as I have enough money I'm quite happy to go and work in a bank or something... I don't care about being rich and famous all my life."

"People think I'm big-headed or weird because I'll go into a newsagent and buy any magazine with a feature about us in it. I read everything about the band, and people forget that if they were in the paper they'd read it too. I do it not because I'm conceited but because I'm proud of the band."

"I was always a bit of a joker at school, and I guess that's why I didn't get any good exam results. I found out very early on that one of the keys to being popular was making the other kids laugh. So that's what I did. I was just this chubby boy who would go around pulling faces and telling jokes and I found myself with a big circle of friends."

"There are a lot of important charities to support, but Aids is really worrying... kids often listen to us when they don't listen to teachers."

"I try not to have any expectations because that way you can never be let down. I'm happy in my world. Mine's a laid-back world – I just go with the flow and see what happens."

"I am so hooked on Nintendo Game Boy that, when I stop playing, my eyes are square and I've got a really bad headache. The only way to feed the addiction is to have another go!"

robbie williams

"Coronation Street is my favourite soap. I like Jack Duckworth best because he never fails to make me laugh. I've never been on the set before but I'd like to be the landlord of the Rover's Return. I'd sit there getting drunk on the pretend beer every night!"

"If I'm home Saturday night I go across the pub. I only go clubbing when I'm in another country. In England, people don't like success, but in Europe you can go out to different places, be a celebrity, and nobody's arsed. It sounds very pop star-ish but that's the truth."

"We try and be entertaining and sometimes we are a little sarcastic, like we will ask a journalist who's a bit slow if he can do joined-up writing. But we don't set out to be rude with our jokes. I mean sarcasm is English wit... Also sometimes in interviews I make things up in answer to people's questions just to keep it interesting, especially when the subject is girls."

"I like the name Rob, but I was nearly called Dominic. Rob means 'fame' in Greek – or that might just be a clever selling ploy of keyring people out there! My confirmation name is Maximillian Colby. I chose that. He was a saint who put himself forward to be called in World War II. My other confirmation name was going to be Mary, but they said I couldn't do that."

"Our stance has always been that we are free from drugs and we are. It's the 90s, find a teenager that hasn't experimented with drugs at my age and I'll shake them by the hand. We couldn't have done the last tour on drugs, I mean I'll have a Pro-Plus and a cup of coffee every now and then. And the reason I won't condemn it is because my ego isn't big enough to say 'don't do this' and 'don't do that'. I find it awful when I read a pop star saying what you should and shouldn't do."

"I am very susceptible to spirits. That might sound a bit silly. I'm not scared of ghosts, I'm just scared of the depression I can feel with tormented spirits. I can never see spirits but I can feel them sometimes breathing down my neck. It's happened in Ireland and Chelmsford and a few other places."

"We've had our clothes ripped off us, jackets going missing, scratches all down our backs – and then we go home to our mums!"

"We get guys laughin' at us all the time. Oh yeah, but they're outnumbered 10:1 by the girls who think it's brill, so there you go."

"I don't think I'm that good-looking and I think that's why I've got this far – everyone took pity on me."

"My mother heard about this audition for a band in a local paper and told me to go along for it, so I did. I remember thinking what a weird bunch of lads they were, and really didn't think we could ever be a band."

"We all wind each other up, but I tend to go that bit further, which is daft of me really."

"There was a time when we'd have been happy with a silver disc – we still would. But to get a double platinum is beyond all our wildest dreams. What we're doing now is like living our dreams. Our dreams have finally come true."

"The July (1993) shows weren't a money-making thing, really. They were to thank the fans for all their support so we gave them six dates. A lot of the money we had already was put into the lighting, rigging etc. And it was such a big show that we could actually have lost money on those concerts."

"We're on £150 a week, and I think that's sufficient... We don't want to go out and buy things really. We've seen people before us go down the hill because of bad money deals and we don't want to be the same... After all, when we're on the road we're working all the time. The record company pays for all the food, travel and accommodation. Having said that, I always spend my £150 dead quick and I'm left with a debt of £200 at the end of a week!"